Claudio Pescio

Pisa
new practical guide

Monumen...
4 itineraries of t...
Useful i...

BET
BONECHI EDIZIONI "IL TURISMO"

The articles on the Museo dell'Opera del Duomo and the Museo delle Sinopie were written by: Antonio Chinca

Reprint 2006

Photos: Bonechi Archives; Paolo Bacherini
          Nicola Grifoni: pages 34 - 35 - 52 - 62 - 63 - 65 - 66 - 67 - 84 - 87 - 88
Layout and cover: Lorenzo Cerrina
Reprohouse: Fotolito Immagine, Florence
Print: Lito Terrazzi, Florence

ISBN 88-7204-350-6

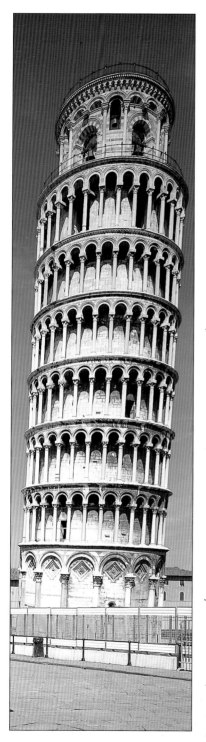

Welcome to Pisa

Unlike the other major art centers of Tuscany, Pisa is practically devoid of great Renaissance monuments for, in fact she made her fortune and accumulated her art treasures mainly during the Middle Ages.

Actually, the peak of Pisa's economic and political power was reached in the 12th-13th centuries when Pisan ships ruled the Tyrrhenian Sea. It was only during this time that the city, whose prosperity came from lucrative trade with the Orient could afford to commission the masterpieces of painting, sculpture, and architecture with which to embellish herself. Foremost among these, is, of course, the Campo dei Miracoli, which after almost a millennium has come down to us practically intact except for its celebrated Campanile, the Leaning Tower of Pisa, which every year that passes, is just a bit more leaning.

But you mustn't make the all too common mistake of thinking that once you've seen the Campo dei Miracoli, you've seen Pisa. In fact our guide is divided into three easy-to-follow and enjoyable itineraries with an appendix for touring the environs so that you don't miss anything. Also, to help you get even more out of your sightseeing, a brief outline of Pisa's history and art history is provided at the beginning.

A BRIEF HISTORY OF PISA

Who founded Pisa is a controversial matter. Some historians believe that the city was colonized by a group of Greeks at the end of the 7th century B.C. Others are convinced that its founders came from nearby Liguria and that it was later settled by the Etruscans. We do know, however, that the city, first an ally of Rome, later became one of her colonies at which time it was re-named *Julia Obsequens*. Under the Emperor Octavian in the 1st century A. D. the *porto pisanus* was enlarged. Although only little of it is extant today, the city's history and prosperity have always been tied in with ports and the sea, for activities connected with the sea have been the mainstay of Pisa's economic life from the very beginning. Seafaring never ceased, not even when the rest of the Italian peninsula was in the throes of terrible crises such as the periods of Roman and barbarian rule and throughout the Longobard dominion. From the outset, Pisa's aim was to build up her fleet and extend her trading and, in fact, she soon became one of the great Mediterranean sea powers. In the 11th century, the Free Commune of Pisa was even able to wrest from the Saracens a good-sized chunk of the Island of Sardina which, as a result, came under Pisan influence in the economic, political, and artistic spheres.

Piazza del Duomo seen from the Porta di Santa Maria.

4

Trajan's Baths, known as Nero's Baths.

The 11th century was a period of fervent artistic activity, especially in architecture when the first examples of the Pisan-Lucchese style appeared. Pisan-Lucchese architecture may best be defined as a local version of the Romanesque, a mixture brewed from different styles and cultures. It not only exerted great influence in the regions of Pisa and Lucca, but went on to affect the architecture of several Mediterranean countries, among them Southern Italy, Corsica, Provence, and, especially, Sardinia. One of the earliest examples of the emerging style is the basilica of San Pietro a Grado, located a few miles from Pisa, which was built at the beginning of the 11th century. A bit later,

in the second half of the 12th century, the cathedral of Pisa, designed by Buscheto, was begun, although it was not finished until the beginning of the 13th century under the direction of Buscheto's successor Rainaldo. This was the period of great prosperity for Pisa, due mainly to intensive trade with the Orient which developed as an offshoot of her active participation in the first Crusade and the alliance she forged with the Normans at the end of the 11th century. The city became at the time the seat of a bishopric whose jurisdiction extended to Sardinia and Corsica. In the 12th century the Pisans joined forces with Emperor Frederick Redbeard, and this led to the annexation of vast territories of Tyrrhenian coast, Calabria, Sicily, and all of Sardinia, as feudal possessions. During these centuries the great names in Pisan art emerged: Bonanno in the 1100s century and Nicola and Giovanni Pisano in the 1200s. The Pisanos, father and son, made Pisan sculpture one of the foremost styles in Italy. In 1173, amidst a hundred difficulties, the Campanile, the famous Leaning Tower, was begun. In the second half of the 13th century, Giovanni di Simone designed the Camposanto Monumentale (cemetery), as well as the churches of Santa Caterina and San Francesco.

His contemporaries in painting, the Pisan masters Francesco Traini and the Master of the Triumph of Death (from the name of the unknown painter's fresco cycle in the Camposanto), were greatly influenced by the Sienese, unlike their successors who would fall more under the sway of Florentine painting. Then, in 1284, the Pisans, whose fleet had in the meantime eclipsed that of another great sea republic, Amalfi, suffered a serious setback when they were soundly beaten by the Genoese at Meloria. This led to a long period of crisis. During the 14th century Pisa's political and eco-

Flag wavers in Piazza Duomo.

The Leaning Tower.

nomic decline was even more pronounced. Deprived of a fleet of her own, she was forced to helplessly look on as Sardinia was conquered by the Aragonese while, at the same time, she was sucked more and more into the sphere of influence of nearby Florence. And, in fact, in 1406, debilitated by a long siege, the Pisans surrendered to the Florentines who thus permanently added Pisa to their dominions. Nevertheless, a slow but steady economic revival marked the next decades. In 1472 the University of Pisa, still a renowned center of learning today, was officially opened and the city enjoyed a brief period of independence, when Charles VIII of France entered Italy in 1494. As soon as the Medicis regained possession of Pisa, they embarked on a number of ambitious building projects, especially in the port area, which went on throughout the 16th and 17th centuries. The Medicis' successors, the Lorraine grand dukes, continued to devote great attention to Pisan affairs. In 1860, Pisa like many other cities of the peninsula, voted to join the newly-founded United Kingdom of Italy. This marked the beginning of Pisa's industrial boom, which soon spread over the whole Pisan region. Unfortunately, the city was not spared the horrors of World War II. One of the monuments which suffered the worst damage, the Camposanto, required years of painstaking restoration before it could be re-opened to the public. Presently a special committee is at work examining various projects for reinforcing the foundations and weight-bearing structures of the famous Leaning Tower.

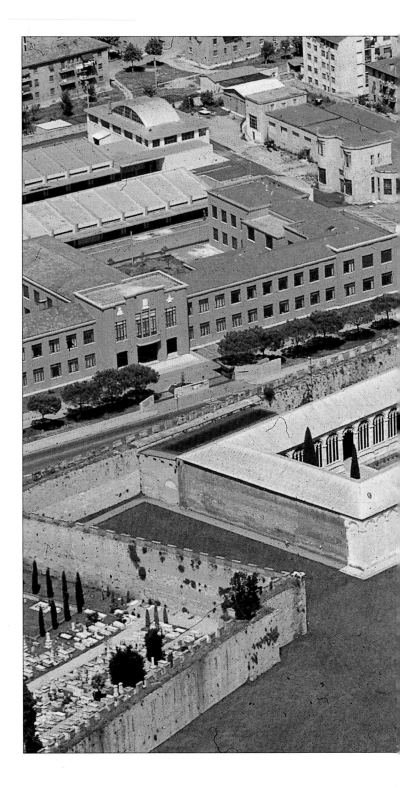

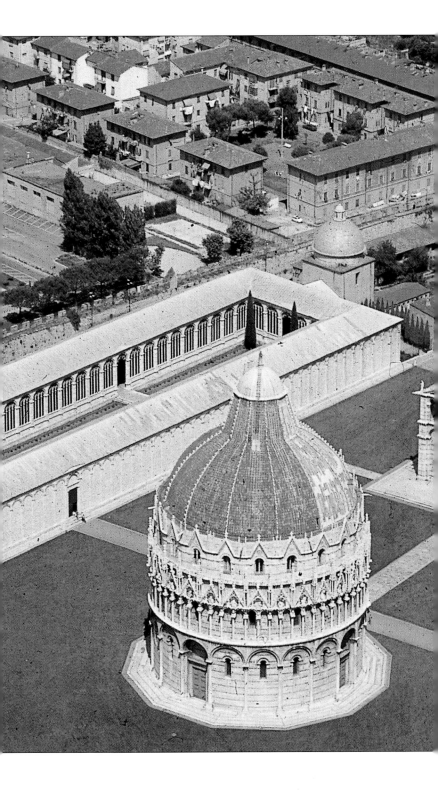

The Camposanto after the bombardement of the World War II.
Preceding page: *the Etruscan lion set atop the Medicean walls.*

FIRST ITINERARY

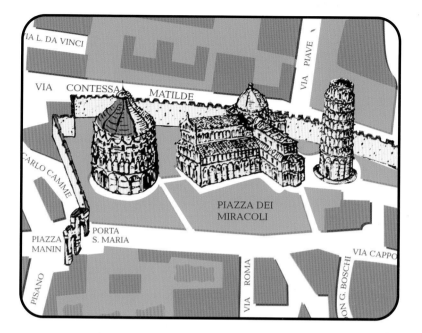

 Campo dei Miracoli

 Cathedral

 Leaning Tower

 Baptistry

 Museo dell'Opera del Duomo

 Camposanto

 Museo delle Sinopie

THE CAMPO DEI MIRACOLI

Pisa's Cathedral Square, known as the Campo dei Miracoli (Square of Miracles) is a veritable miracle of architectural achievement. Four buildings, the Cathedral, Leaning Tower, Baptistry, and Camposanto, beautifully shown off on their lawn setting, form one of the outstanding architectural complexes in all of Italy. Their striking stylistic harmony is even more amazing if one considers that it took three hundred years to build them, naturally under the supervision of different architects. Over the centuries few major changes have been wrought, and today we can enjoy the Campo dei Miracoli in all its original splendor.

THE CATHEDRAL

Work on the cathedral was begun in 1064 under the direction of Buscheto (or Buschetto), originally believed to have been Greek, and now known to have been a native Pisan. His mortal remains rest in a simple urn placed behind the first arch on the lefthand side of the façade marked by a commemorative stone. The unfinished building was consecrated in 1118 by Pope Gelasius II. In the 12th century the façade, designed by Rainaldo, was erected, although construction went on for centuries more. The cathedral, exerted enormous influence on countless other architectural designs, not only in Pisa, but all over Tuscany and Sardinia as well.

THE EXTERIOR

The cathedral is completely faced with precious colored marbles. The lower section of the five-register façade is divided into seven zones by blind arcading. Alternate losenge and circle designs, inlaid with exquisite geometric patterns,

The façade of the Cathedral.
Preceding page: ***Piazza dei Miracoli.***
Following pagesi: ***the Cathedral and the Leaning Tower.***

set off the arches. The columns framing the main portal, unlike those of the secondary portals, are completely carved with an intricate acanthus leaf pattern. The mosaics in the portal lunettes date from the 1400s but were radically altered in the 19th century. Their subjects are St. Reparata (left), the *Assumption* of the *Virgin* (center) and *St John the Baptist* (right). The late 16th century bronze doors by followers of Giambologna were built to replace Bonanno's originals of 1186 which perished in a fire. The scenes depicted on the main portal are episodes from the *life of the Virgin*, while the other two recount the *life of Christ*. The upper façade has four rows of Lombard-style arcading. On the corners of the second row are statues of *evangelists*, while a statue of the *Virgin and Child*, by Andrea Pisano, and two *angels*, by followers of Giovanni Pisano, look down from the summit. The arcading and ornamental motifs of the façade are continued along the sides

Virgin and child, the statues at the top of the cathedral façade.
Opposite page: **detail of the losenge decorations on the apse of the cathedral.**

The central door of the Cathedral.

of the building. Going to the back of the church at the point where the apse and transept meet on the Leaning Tower side is **Porta di San Ranieri** which serves as the present-day entrance to the cathedral. The bronze doors of 1180, masterpieces by Bonanno, are divided into twenty compartments in which the *life of Christ* is depicted in an extraordinary vigorous style,

influenced by the three-dimensional quality of the Romanesque master, Wiligelmo, though not devoid of Byzantine influxes either. The stylistic unity of the architecture is maintained in the apse, which has blind arcading surmounted by two rows of loggias. The unusual elliptical dome rising over the crossing was built in 1380 by Lupo di Gante and Puccio di Gadduccio. It rests

*The lunette over the central door with the Madonn*a by Giuseppe di Modena da Lucca; below: *detail of the capitals.*

26

Preceding page: *the St. Ranieri Door by Bonanno Pisano.*
On this page: *two panels from the St. Ranieri Door with Scenes from the Life of Christ* by Bonanno Pisano.

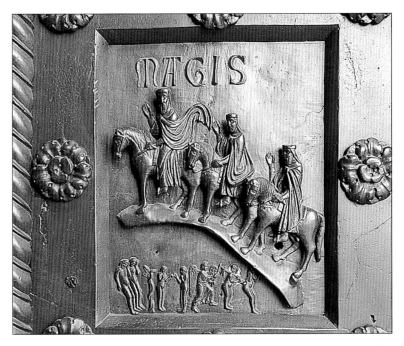

upon an octagonal drum and is set off by a graceful Gothic gallery.

THE INTERIOR OF THE CATHEDRAL

The double aisles of the stately interior are marked by plain granite columns with Corinthian capitals. The upper galleries on either side of the nave, called matronei, were reserved for female worshippers. The striped marble facing repeats the pattern of the exterior decoration and adds a lively coloristic note to the solemn procession of arches along the aisles and matronei. Towering over the crossing of the aisled transept and the nave is the dome which rests upon Arab-style pointed arches. The **pulpit** in the nave, sculpted by Giovanni Pisano

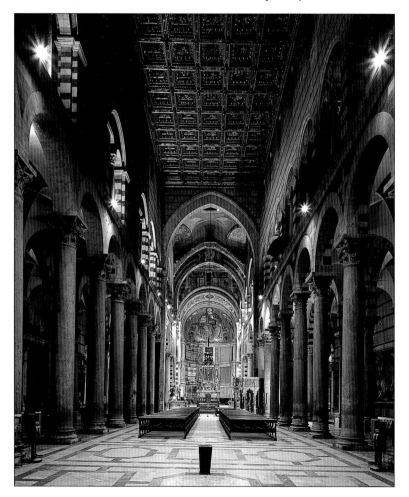

The interior of the Cathedral.
Opposite page: *the pulpit* by Giovanni Pisano.

between 1302 and 1310, is universally considered the master's finest work and ranks as one of the greatest sculptures of the Italian Gothic. Dismantled after a fire in 1599, it was recomposed and placed in its present location in 1926. Unlike the earlier versions of carved pulpits which were polygonal, Giovanni's is practically round. The pulpit proper is supported by allegorical statues and columns, two of which rest on crouching lions. The statues in the middle are personifications of *Theological Virtues*. The sculpted panels around the sides are New Testament scenes, skillfully rendered to exploit the maximum of dramatic tension. The scenes, each of which is animated by a host of

Two details of the pulpit panels portraying: the Nativity (above)
and *the Crucifixion* (below).
Opposite page: *the Caryatid Figures.*

gesticulating figures, represent the *Birth of Christ, the Annunciation, the Visitation, the Nativity, the Adoration of the Magi, the Presentation in the Temple, the Flight into Egypt, the Slaughter of the Innocents, the Kiss of Judas, the Crucifixion,* and *the Last Judgment.* In the center of the nave is a 16th century chandelier, popularly known as **Galileo's Lamp** since, according to tradition, the great Pisan scientist figured out the law of pendulum movement by observing it swinging back and forth. At the far end of the righthand transept is the **Chapel of San Ranieri**, inside of which is an urn containing St. Ranieri's relics. Above is a 15th century Sienese mosaic of a *Virgin in Glory.* In the left aisle is the **tomb of the Emperor of Luxembourg, Harold VII**, the "alto Arrigo" (tall Harry) mentioned in Dante's Divine Comedy. The tomb of the Emperor, who died in Buonconvento near Siena, was sculpted by the 14th century

The tomb of Henry VII of Luxembourg; below: *the Urn of St.Ranieri.*
Preceding page: *Galileo's Lamp.*

master, Tino da Camaino. Below the figure of the emperor is a frieze with the *12 apostles*. The two angels in the niche were frescoed in the 1400s by Ghirlandaio.

The huge figure of **Christ enthroned** between the *Virgin* and *St. John the Evangelist* wholly dominates the choir zone of the church. The mosaic dates from the early 14th century and clearly bears strong Byzantine influence. The figure of St. John, noteworthy for it sensitive treatment of light and shade, is a late work – possibly the last – of the great Florentine master, Cimabue. The superb painting of **St. Agnes with a lamb** (on the righthand pillar in the choir) is by the 16th century Florentine master, Andrea del Sarto. The melancholy figure of the saint is set against a

St. Agnes by Andrea del Sarto.

Christ Enthroned, detail of the mosaic over the apse of the Cathedral.

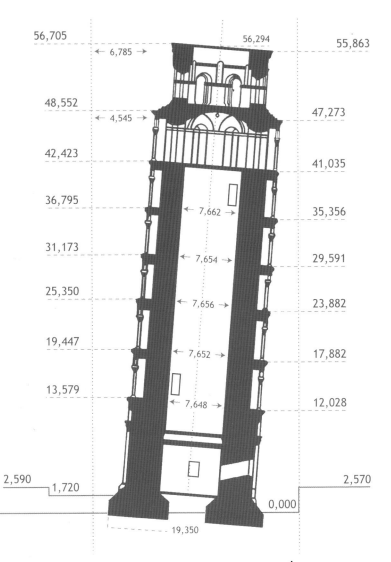

56,705

56,294

55,863

← 6,785 →

48,552

47,273

← 4,545 →

42,423

41,035

36,795

35,356

← 7,662 →

31,173

29,591

← 7,654 →

25,350

23,882

← 7,656 →

19,447

17,882

← 7,652 →

13,579

12,028

← 7,648 →

2,590

2,570

1,720

0,000

← 19,350 →

Cross section of the Belltower. Opposite page: *the Leaning Tower.*

Leonardesque landscape. Above the triumphal arch is a *Virgin and Child*, attributed to the master of San Torpè and dated c. 1300. On the altar of the little chapel to the left of the choir is a 13th century painting, the *Madonna di Sotto gli Organi.*

THE LEANING TOWER

Famous world over, it has come to be the symbol of Pisa.

Unfortunately, its inclination, now 4.265 meters (13.694 feet), is increasing at the slow but preoccupying rate of 1 mm a year. Research on static problems relating to the monument is currently underway, with the hope that a solution may be found before it is too late. The tower is 179 feet tall on the north side and 177 feet on the south side. From the top, where Galileo pedormed his experiments on falling masses in the 16th century, visitors can enjoy a splendid view of the city and the countryside around Pisa.

The belltower was begun in 1173, probably under the supervision of Bonanno. When three floors were already up, the terrain on the south side showed the first signs of sinking and work had to be suspended. In 1273 the project was resumed by Giovanni di Simone, although it was not completed until the second half of the 14th century by Tommaso Pisano, son of Andrea. The tower is cylindrical, a shape to be found in earlier belltowers in Ravenna on the east coast. Like the cathedral façade, it has a row of blind arches surmonted by loggias which give the massive building a delicate, airy appearance. The bellchamber on the top has blind arches alternating with round arch openings. The *Virgin and Child* in the lunette over the entrance was sculpted by Andrea Guardi.

Above: *the belfry in the Leaning Tower.*
Preceding page: *detail of the Leaning Tower.*

THE BAPTISTRY

When plans for the baptistry were drawn up by Diotisalvi in 1152, both the architectural design and building materials were selected to harmonize with the style of the cathedral, at the time under construction a few yards away. Work progressed slowly but steadily under the supervision of such masters as Nicola and Giovanni Pisano, and was finally completed towards the end of the 14th century.

The Baptistry. Opposite page: ***detail of the loggia*** decorated by Nicola Pisano.

THE EXTERIOR

The continuous blind arcading that encircles the round building is broken up by four portals. The main portal (the one with carved pillars on the cathedral side) is adorned with 13th century reliefs illustrating stories from the *life of St. John the Baptist* in the architrave. The *Ascension*, figures of the *Apostles*, and the *months* decorate the jambs. The statue of the *Virgin* in the lunette is a copy of Giovanni Pisano's original, now preserved in the Camposanto. The loggia of the second level is surmounted by gable-shaped cusps and pinnacles adorned with sculpture by the Pisanos and their pupils. The dome, divided into eight sections by sculpted marble ribbing, strikingly crowns the building. On top is a gigantic bronze statue of *St. John the Baptist* dating from the early 1400s.

The baptismal font by Guido Bigarelli da Como *with the statue of St. John the Baptist* by Italo Griselli.
Preceding pages: *Piazza dei Miracoli with the Baptistry in the foreground.*

THE INTERIOR

The spacious interior is divided into a central zone surmounted by a matroneo and an outer ambulatory marked by a circle of massive pillars. Inside, the dome is pyramidal. At the center is the huge *baptismal font* faced with superb inlaid marble and relief panels executed by Guido Bigarelli from Como in 1246, The bronze statue of *St. John the Baptist* set on a Byzantine capital is a modern work. To the left is

Nicola Pisano's celebrated **pulpit** of 1260. Hexagonal, it is sustained by seven columns, three of which rest on crouching lions. The panels, sculpted in bas-relief, represent the *Nativity, the Adoration of the Magi, the Presentation at the Temple, the Crucifixion, and the Last Judgment.* The sculpture of Nicola Pisano, father of Giovanni, represents the link between Romanesque and Gothic. Nicola's figures and compositions were undoubtedly

The interior of the Baptistry.

Two details of the pulpit panels portraying the Presentation in the Temple (above) and *the Adoration of the Magi* (below).
Opposite page: *the Baptistry pulpit.*

greatly influenced by Roman sculpture to which he was constantly exposed, as numerous carved sarcophagi were still extant in medieval Pisa. Along the walls are several sculptures which were once part of the exterior decoration.

THE MUSEO DELL'OPERA DEL DUOMO

The building that houses the Museo dell'Opera del Duomo stands on the southwest corner of the grassy and solitary Piazza dei Miracoli. The view from the upper loggia extending around the ancient cloister is truly spectacular. It creates a wonderful visual and emotional link with the artworks housed here and the monuments from which they originated.

The buildings, originally erected as the residence for the cathedral's canons (who lived there from about 1100 to the early XVII century) was later used for different purposes. Its current configuration dates from the early seventeenth century when it was completely remodelled to house the Seminario Arcivescovile. Later it passed to private ownership, then in 1784 it became the headquarters of the academy of fine arts, and home of Giovanni Rosini, great man of let-

Portico of the museum with the busts from the outer loggia of the Baptistry.

ters. In 1887 it was taken over by the Cappuccine Sisters and became a cloistered convent.

Finally, in 1979 it was purchased by the Opera della Primaziale in order to create a true Museo dell'Opera. It was opened in 1986, and through its treasures and artworks, it tells visitors the long and complex story of the Primaziale Pisana and its famous monuments together with the city's cultural and artistic history.

The oldest and most famous nucleus of the museum's collections are located on the ground floor and in the portico. These are sculptures from the XII to XVII century, including the masterpieces by Nicola and Giovanni Pisano, Tino di Camaino and Nino Pisano. The *Tesoro del Duomo*, or Cathedral Treasure, is in a separate room and in the adjacent chapel. It comprises liturgical items and precious objects from the Medieval cathedral including Giovanni Pisano's ivory

Madonna and silverware dating from the XVI to XIX centuries. The rest of the museum is arranged more or less in chronological and systematic order: on the first floor there are sculptures dating from the XVI to the XIX centuries, wooden intarsias from the Renaissance, illuminated Medieval choir-books, sacred paraments, liturgical garments and cloths, a collection of Egyptian, Etruscan and Roman objects and finally a graphic section with famous XIX century engravings by Carlo Lasinio, first curator of the Camposanto Monumentale (the Monumental Cemetery).

THE ISLAMIC BRONZES: THE GRIFFON AND THE BASIN

The relationships between Pisa, the maritime city and the

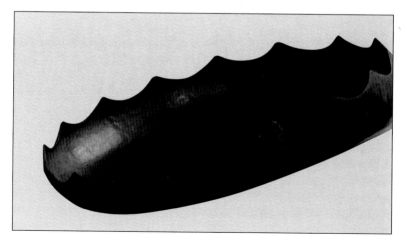

Bronze basin.

Fatimid Griffon (XII century).

Orient, land of the heathens was always difficult, strife ridden, and yet there was always secret admiration which can be symbolized in the Islamic items that are believed to have been captured as war booty.

The echo of the great voyages to the East, of relations with a dis-tant, alien world, the memory of fierce battles and long military expeditions, but al so perhaps of peaceful trade are clearly heard in these items that are displayed not only as victory trophies but also as special souvenirs. They are a lasting remembrance of important and valuable contacts with a cul-

Headless female statue by Giovanni Pisano (XIV century).

The Virgin of the Smile. Opposite page: ***the Ivory Madonna.***

turally rich civilization.

It is in this light that the two Islamic pieces should be viewed and studied, they are the cast *bronze basin* and *Fatimid griffon.*

The griffon is a monumental statue dating from the XII century, and up until the late XIX cen-

tury it stood atop the typanum of the cathedral's apse, that is the most important and visually striking position for those who came to the heart of the city. Little is known about this superb piece. And it matters less if it was taken as booty during the crusades, during the Balearic expedition or if it was the gift of some Arabian prince. One thing is sure, its powerful shape is typical of Iranian Islamic art.

The other famous piece is the metal basin with the fine engraved decorations. There are inscriptions along the edge and zoomorphic figures in medallions. It too is very old and perhaps dates from Seljuk dynasty (XII century); it is exceptionally crafted and is the focus of great attention for scholars in this field.

THE HEADLESS FEMALE STATUES

Giovanni Pisano's artistic skill virtually bursts from the two Verrucano marble blocks carved into the figures of two headless girls.

The first is a beautiful female figure holding a vase in her left hand; the right arm is missing. The forms are balanced and move around a vertical axis that supports the figure as she steps forward. It is harmonious and light, with a uniquely graceful sense of motion.

The other statue is vibrant with life, spontaneity and movement. Giovanni's mastery comes through as the girl slightly raises her skirts to dance.

THE VIRGIN OF THE SMILE

This may be one of Giovanni Pisano's earliest carvings of the Virgin (1280 circa). It reveals a. clear break with the classic dignity and serene solemnity of Nicola Pisano's style, and a definite Gothic imprint.

The Infant Jesus, is absorbed in a loving, silent coversation with His Mother. Her arm holds him safety and the entire motion of the statue seems to be directing his gaze upwards.

It was with the subject of the silent conversations of gazes (hence statue's other title the Virgin of the Conservation) that Giovanni Pisano managed to imbue the relationship between the Mother and Son with new psychological and spiritual

This is how the elegant profile of this Madonna represents the most plastic, human and definite expression of a Mother who adores her child and in turn is loved by him.

THE IVORY MADONNA

The Ivory Madonna, carved by Giovanni Pisano around the end of the XIII century is one of the most famous and prized works in the museum.

By cleverly using the natural curves of the elephant tusk, the artist managed to create a highly dynamic sculpture without diminishing its stately-sacred meaning. In fact the dynamism blends perfectly with the refined elegance of the artist's mastery.

THE WOODEN CHRIST FROM THE CATHEDRAL

This monumental colored wood carving of Christ is truly worthy of admiration. Until the disastrous fire of 1595 it hung in the cathedral presbytry.

It is probably datable around the second half of the XII century and can certainly be identified as a Deposed Christ. It was part of a group similar to the ones in the Pieve at Vicopisano and in the Volterra cathedral.

Notwithstanding an old legend reported by Pisan historians saying that the Christ was brought from the Holy Land, this magnificent crucified figure, with its stark beauty and lines requiring little decoration, is French.

It is one of the greatest masterpieces of period sculpture, especially for its fine proportions and shapes. It possesses a charm of its own which is accentuated by the contrast between the plastic masses of diagonal broken rhythms that delineate Christ's body against the cross giving it drama and pathos, and the fine, subtle sculpting seemingly carved with the tip of a chisel that delicately embroiders the surface.

It is sufficient to note the decided and elegant folds of the loin-cloth, the ribs that are just visible on the chest, and the solemn face, filled with humanity's suffering. Then there is a clear contrast with the stylized lines of the elongated limbs. All this makes it easier to understand that this Deposed Crhist, with its majestic, solemn beauty, with its profound asceticism and spirituality can be classed among the masterpieces of Burgundian sculpture.

The Wooden Christ from the Cathedral.

THE CAMPOSANTO

The Camposanto is the rectangular structure running practically the whole length of the north side of the square. The exterior is decorated with the same blind arch pattern used on the other buildings. Over one of the two simple entrances is an elegant Gothic tabernacle by followers of Giovanni Pisano. The Camposanto was begun by Giovanni di

On top: *the tabernacle of the Camposanto*.
above: *the exterior*.

Simone in 1277. It was built so that the mortal remains of the Pisans could be buried in the precious earth from the Holy Land that archbishop Ubaldo de' Lanfranchi had actually commissioned the Pisan fleet to transport from Golgotha. In July 1944 the cemetery was so badly bombed that its lead roof caved in and fused, - in some cases irreparable damage - to the frescoes, sculptures, and sarcophagi beneath the rubble. The restoration of these treasures was only completed in 1979. Now most of the frescoes have been put back in their original places and their sinopias (underlying preparatory sketches) are on view in a special little museum in the nearby Spedale.

THE INTERIOR

Majestic, yet peaceful, the courtyard of the Camposanto, with its simple lawn and paired cypress trees, gives one the impression of being in a cloister. The Roman sarcophagi and funerary monuments set along the corridors, previously

scattered about the Campo dei Miracoli, mostly in the area around the cathedral, were placed here at the turn of the century. Most of them date from the Hellenistic or Early Christian periods. Decorated with reliefs of mythological scenes, they were often re-used for the burial of Pisan nobles between the 12th and 15th centuries. A few are even of great artistic value. Three outstanding examples are the sarcophagus with scenes from the *myth of Phedra* (2nd century AD), the so-called *Wedding Sarcophagus*, and the *sarcophagus of the Muses* (3rd century AD), all of which are in the north corridor. There are also monu-

The courtyard inside the Camposanto with the Dal Pozzo Chapel.

ments dating from later periods, such as the *tomb of Archbishop Schelatti* by Nino Pisano (1363), the *tomb of the della Gherardesca family* by a pupil of Giovanni Pisano (1320), as well as others by Ammannati, Tribolo (16th century), and even more recent ones by Dupré and Lorenzo Bartolini (19th century).

The frescoes, however, are the highlight of the Camposanto. In the south corridor are stories from the *Old Testament* by Benozzo Gozzoli (15th century), unfortunately in very poor condition. The 14th century frescoes illustrating stories from the *lives of St. Ranieri* and *Job* are by Taddeo Gaddi.

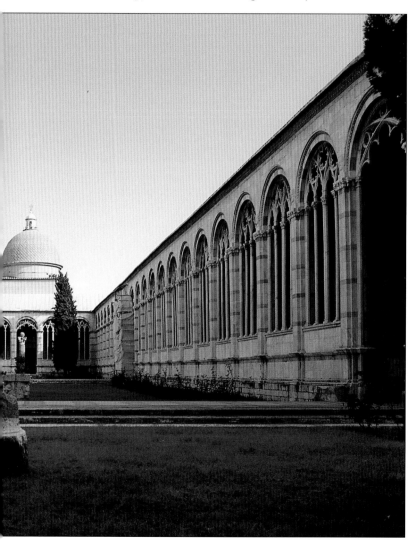

Roman sarcophagus; below: *classic sarcophagus with scenes from the story of Phaedra and Hippolytus* (Northern Gallery).
Opposite page, from top: *two statues in the Northern Gallery* and *the chains of the ancient city's harbor.*

Detail of the Triumph of Death, with the scenes of the Cavalcade.
Opposite page: *detail of the Stories of the Anacorite hermits*, by the Master of
the Triumph of Death.

Opposite, in the north corridor, are late 14th century frescoes by Piero di Puccio with cosmological motifs and episodes from *Genesis*.

Entering the Cappella Ammannati, we turn left into the **Salone degli Affreschi** (fresco hall) which contains the *Triumph of Death, the Last Judgment, Hell,* and *stories of the Anacorite hermits*. This remarkable fresco cycle, painted in the 14th century, is a complex narration of great dramatic effect. Undoubtedly, the *Triumph of Death* is the most remarkable of all.

The drama of the scenes is played up by the striking use of composition, while no detail is considered unworthy of being described. Although art historians have made countless attributions, including Traini, Orcagna, Buffalmacco, and Lorenzetti, the name of the master who painted it is still a mystery. To the right of the Cappella Ammannati is a photographic exhibition of the Camposanto frescoes before the July 1944 disaster. Returning to the north corridor, we find other frescoes, the *story of Noah* by Piero di Puccio and the *Grape harvest* by Benozzo Gozzoli.

AB 5519808

TRENITALIA
SELF SERVICE

BIGLIETTO
TRENO ORDINARIO
DA CONVALIDARE

N. 1 ADULTI

UTILIZZABILE DAL 09/06/08 AL 08/08/08

Partenza	- - - >Arrivo		Classe
FIRENZE	PISA CENTRALE		2

VIA EMPOLI*

KM 81

TARIFFA INTERA TAR.39/01
VALE 6H DA CONVALIDA

EUR *****5,40
CARTA CREDITO
P.IVA 0540315I003

TOT.BIGL.N. 2

0749AB5519808

00178 6004 ROMA TERMINI   090608 21:21 01417-515

CONDIZIONI DI TRASPORTO

Il contratto di trasporto è disciplinato per i collegamenti nazionali dalle "Condizioni e Tariffe per il trasporto delle persone sulle FS" e per quelli internazionali dalla "Convenzione relativa ai trasporti internazionali per Ferrovia."

Maggiori informazioni su "condizioni di trasporto" e "modalità di convalida del biglietto" presso le biglietterie delle stazioni, le agenzie di viaggio e sul sito www.ferroviedellostato.it/trenitalia per i passeggeri/area clienti/condizioni di trasporto.

MODALITÀ DI CONVALIDA DEL BIGLIETTO

Prima della partenza convalidare alla obliteratrice i biglietti:

- senza prenotazione del posto: abbonamenti e biglietti per treni Regionali, Espressi, Intercity e Intercity Notte. La validità, secondo la tariffa utilizzata, decorre dal momento della convalida del biglietto.

- con prenotazione del posto se utilizzati, nei termini previsti dalla tariffa utilizzata, su treni diversi da quello originariamente prenotato.

In entrambi i casi, i viaggiatori con biglietto non convalidato incorrono nel pagamento di penalità. Nel caso non fosse possibile convalidare i biglietti per mancanza o guasto delle obliteratrici, rivolgersi, all'atto della salita, al personale di bordo che convaliderà il biglietto senza applicare alcuna penalità.

AB 5519807

TRENITALIA
SELF SERVICE

BIGLIETTO CON PRENOTAZIONE
EUROSTAR ITALIA
STANDARD

N. 1 ADULTI

DA ESIBIRE IN CASO DI CAMBIO TRENO

Data	Ora	Partenza	- - - >Arrivo	Data	Ora	Classe
21.06	07.30	ROMA TERMINI	FIRENZE S.M.N.	21.06	09.06	2

TRENO 9428   CARROZZA 009   POSTI 36 FINESTRINO

TARIFFA STANDARD EUROSTAR

TOT.BIGL.N.2   EUR ****38,0'
                                               CARTA CREDITO
                    83096766Ø123   P.IVA Ø54Ø315100З
                    Ø749AB5519807   PNR:LTC4YR CP:676601
ØØ177 6ØØ4 ROMA TERMINI   Ø9Ø6Ø8 21:21 1417 - 515

CONDIZIONI DI TRASPORTO

Il contratto di trasporto è disciplinato per i collegamenti nazionali dalle "Condizioni e Tariffe per il trasporto delle persone sulle FS" e per quelli internazionali dalla "Convenzione relativa ai trasporti internazionali per Ferrovia."

Maggiori informazioni su "condizioni di trasporto" e "modalità di convalida del biglietto" presso le biglietterie delle stazioni, le agenzie di viaggio e sul sito www.ferroviedellostato.it/trenitalia per i passeggeri/area clienti/condizioni di trasporto.

MODALITÀ DI CONVALIDA DEL BIGLIETTO

Prima della partenza convalidare alla obliteratrice i biglietti:

* senza prenotazione del posto: abbonamenti e biglietti per treni Regionali, Espressi, Intercity e Intercity Notte. La validità, secondo la tariffa utilizzata, decorre dal momento della convalida del biglietto.

* con prenotazione del posto se utilizzati, nei termini previsti dalla tariffa utilizzata, su treni diversi da quello originariamente prenotato.

In entrambi i casi, i viaggiatori con biglietto non convalidato incorrono nel pagamento di penalità. Nel caso non fosse possibile convalidare i biglietti per mancanza o guasto delle obliteratrici, rivolgersi, all'atto della salita, al personale di bordo che convaliderà il biglietto senza applicare alcuna penalità.

AB 5588710

TRENITALIA
SELF SERVICE
UTILIZZABILE DAL 15/06/08 AL 14/08/08

BIGLIETTO
TRENO ORDINARIO
DA CONVALIDARE

N. 1 ADULTI

Partenza	- - - Arrivo		Classe
ROMA TERMINI	FRASCATI		2

VIA RD CASIA

KM 24
TARIFFA INTERA TAR.39/01
VALE 6H DA CONVALIDA

TOT.BIGL.N. 1

EUR *****1,90
CARTA CREDITO
P.IVA 05403281003

00005 6043 ROMA TERMINI 150608 00:19 01417-525
0749AB5588710

CONDIZIONI DI TRASPORTO

Il contratto di trasporto è disciplinato per i collegamenti nazionali dalle "Condizioni e Tariffe per il trasporto delle persone sulle FS" e per quelli internazionali dalla "Convenzione relativa ai trasporti internazionali per Ferrovia."

Maggiori informazioni su "condizioni di trasporto" e "modalità di convalida del biglietto" presso le biglietterie delle stazioni, le agenzie di viaggio e sul sito www.ferroviedellostato.it/trenitalia per i passeggeri/area clienti/condizioni di trasporto.

MODALITÀ DI CONVALIDA DEL BIGLIETTO

Prima della partenza convalidare alla obliteratrice i biglietti:

* senza prenotazione del posto: abbonamenti e biglietti per treni Regionali, Espressi, Intercity e Intercity Notte. La validità, secondo la tariffa utilizzata, decorre dal momento della convalida del biglietto.

* con prenotazione del posto se utilizzati, nei termini previsti dalla tariffa utilizzata, su treni diversi da quello originariamente prenotato.

In entrambi i casi, i viaggiatori con biglietto non convalidato incorrono nel pagamento di penalità. Nel caso non fosse possibile convalidare i biglietti per mancanza o guasto delle obliteratrici, rivolgersi, all'atto della salita, al personale di bordo che convaliderà il biglietto senza applicare alcuna penalità.

THE MUSEUM OF
THE SINOPIAS

The Museum of the Sinopias is currently housed in a wing of the old Ospedale di Misericordia thttwas built to designs by Giovanni di Simone between 1257 and 1286, before the monu-

A curious historical episode, that took place on the Tyrrhenian coast in 1241 is closely linked to the construction of this hospital. Some ships that were carrying cardinals to Rome for a conclave the pope had called in order to depose the Emperor Frederick II were captured by the Ghibelline fleet. Therefore the pope, Gregory IX, excommunicated the

Entrance to the museum.

mental cemetry. Then it was expanded during the first half of the XIV century along the south side of Piazza del Duomo.

entire city; his writ was only revoked when the Pisans laid the first stone of the hospital to repent publicly for their grave error.

The Wedding of Isaac and Rebecca, by Benozzo Gozzoli.

Although the building was greatly remodelled over the years, and mainly in the XIX century, it is still fascinating. The long, broad, brick and stone facade completes the perspective of Piazza dei Miracoli, and comprises an elegant setting for the rows of stalls filled with colorful wares that attract tourists seeking souvenirs of the city.

After considerable restorations that have preserved and maintained the building's original structure, the existing museum was inaugurated in 1979. It contains the sinopias from the monumental cemetery.

Sinopias are the preparatory drawings for frescoes done directly on the wall; one of the explanations for the development of this technique is the lack of large quantities of paper or other similar materials during the XIV century.

The drawings were done in small size, directly onto the next to the last coat of plaster called "arricciato".

The artists used a brush dipped into a red-earth pigment (actually they also used greenish yellow pigments and charcoal)

Stories of Abraham and Hagar, by Benozzo Gozzoli.
Opposite page: *Anacorite hermits,* by the Master of the Triumph of Death.

from Sinope, a city in Asia Minor, and hence the name "sinopia".

These drawings were then covered with a layer of rough and fine sand called "grassello" onto which the colors were applied. When the work was complete sinopias, evidently were permanently hidden.

They became visible following a tragic event. During War II, an incendiary bomb exploded on the Campo on the night of 27 July 1944. The ensuing fire destroyed most of the frescoes; the few that remained were in such poor condition that they had to be removed for restoration. As they were being taken off, the lovely preliminary drawings once again saw the light. Now, using the same techniques applied in fresco restoration, the sinopias are fixed onto eternit slabs and are displayed in a separate gallery.

The sinopias are extremely important in terms of Medieval art because they were done by the great masters themselves. The frescoes, on the other hand, were actually painted by the masters' pupils and assistants.

The sinopias, therefore, are expressive and free, they have a freshness of line and spontaneity of composition and execution that are the tangible fruits of great artistic talent.

THE UPPER FLOOR

The museum is arranged on two levels: the upper is dedicated to the panels with the most interesting and oldest sinopias, that is the *Holy Fathers*, the *Last Judgement, Hell* and the famous "*Triumph of Death*". They were all done by an unknown artist dubbed the "Master of the Triumph of Death". His true identity, Buonamico Buffalmacco was discovered by the art critic Luciano Bellosi in the 'fifties.

This great Florentine artist drew his figures with a firm hand that made elegant, clean lines. In the long panel of the Triumph of Death, they seem to spring from the rough plaster surface. It is sufficient to look at the purity of the expression on the faces, the fine outlines of the horses and other animals, the great battle between the angels and demons to understand that we are looking at the work of a truly great artist. In the

rather uniform panorama of fourteenth century painting that was dominated by Giotto's influence, Buffalmacco seems tohstruck out on his own, instead of blindly following the great master 's rules, and thereby partially renewed the traditions by working from within. It is interesting to compare the sinopia with the fresco. One can see the changes, the artist's "second opinion", details that were eliminated in the final version. In brief, the whole, painstaking process of fresco. and sketch are there, the basis of a fresco cycle the zenith of the Medieval world's artistic achievement.

This impression is confirmed by looking at the sinopias of the *Ascension*, with the traditional Christ in the mandorla, carried by four angels. In the drawing the figure has a spiritual and yet profoundly human beauty and a severe grace that was partly hidden by the colors added when the fresco was painted.

The sinopia of the *Crucifixion* is located on the eastern wall on the same floor. It was the first great fresco cycle (1320-30) by the Pisan artist Francesco Traini. Although the central part of the sinopia is missing, the composition is still clearly legible. A careful analysis reveals the artist's great skill acquired through lessons from Simone Martini and Lippo Memmi perhaps even more than the finished fresco.

It is sufficient to look at the figure of Christ on the Cross. It

The groundfloor room.

was drawn diagonally to add strength to the composition, and the facial features. Even in death they remained gentle, the face is drooping on the chest; th stomach is drawn in to emphasize the suffering. The angels with spread wings, are blinded with pain and seem to flutter madly around the Cross. Below, the figures of the onlookers, drawn with curving, continuous lines not to break up the rhythms, seem to participate in, this great collective drama.

On the northern wall, there are small sinopias by four of the greatest painters who worked in Florence during the XIV century. Taddeo Gaddi was Giotto's favourite pupil, and althrough he continued with the master's pictorial lines, he did additional studies on perspective and created the *Stories of Job*. Andrea Bonaiuti, created the *Storie of St. Ranier*; Spinello Aretino painted the *Stories of St. Efisio and Potito*. He was still a member of Giotto's school, but the fourteenth century was drawing to a close, and he continued by enlivening the tradition with brilliant innovations. The fourth great artist was Antonio Veneziano who developed an intelligent bond between the traditional school of Giotto and the Bolognese world of miniature.

The collection on the upper floor ends with the large sinopia of the *Ptolemaic Cosmography*, that is the Birth of the Universe. It is presented in a series of concentric circles clearly influence by Ptolemy and Augustine; it was executed by Piero di Puccio da Orvieto, an artist known solely for his fresco cycle in the Campo Santo (the drawings for the *Coronation of the Vrgin* and the first *Stories of Genesis*) can be seen on the ground floor. These works reveal his brilliant taste for architectural compositions where careful attenti on to space and proportions blends with strange deformities in the perspective.

The sinopias by Benozzo Gozzoli are located on the groundfloor; these works are totally different as to nature and meaning when compared with those on the first floor.

By the time Gozzoli was painting, paper was much more readily available; therefore, artists no longer had to draw sinopias directly onto the wall.

The wall thus became an enormous sketchbook, where the master and his pupils "jotted down" their ideas for the arrangement and composition of the fresco.

This is why these sinopias are particularly fascinating: they are sketches filled with references to daily life. They transport us back in time and provide priceless information about the artist's techniques. He used mathematics and geometry to develop the large, complex perspective, and also to outline the human figures.

The tour of the museum ends with an interesting collection of watercolored drawings by Giampaolo Lasinio, son of the Monumental Cemetery's first curator . These pictures give a clear and precise idea of what Europe's greatest XIV and XV fresco cycle looked like before it was damaged.

SECOND ITINERARY

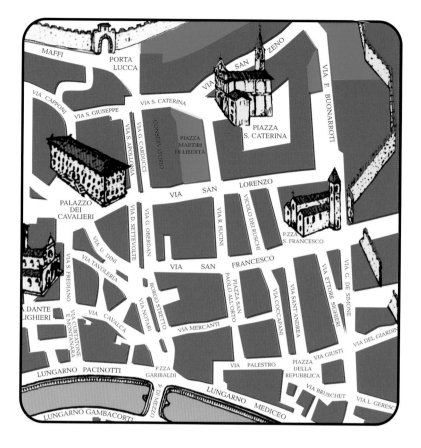

Ponte di Mezzo

Church of
San Francesco

University

Church of
Santa Caterina

Piazza dei
Cavalieri

Museo
Nazionale di
San Matteo

This itinerary starts off from a bridge. **Ponte di Mezzo**, focal point of Pisan life since time immemorial. On the right bank of the Arno, the bridge comes out in Piazza Garibaldi. From the square, we turn left into Lungarno Pacinotti and continue along the river. After making a brief pause at the celebrated *Caffè dell'Ussero*, opened in 1794,

on the ground floor of a 15th century palace, **Palazzo Agostini**, we turn right into Via Curtatone e Montanara. The **University of Pisa**, also known as La Sapienza (the Learned), is on this street. Although its façade is modern, the building dates back to the 15th century, while the university itself is even older (it is believed to have

Palazzo Agostini.

been in existence since the 1100s). Throughout the centuries one of the foremost institutions of higher learning in Italy, Pisa University is still a center of great international renown today.

Proceeding, we soon come to the **church of San Frediano**, set in a little square on our left. Originally built in the 11th-12th centuries, it was greatly altered in the 1600s. The façade is quite simple, with the typical Pisan arcading in the lower section and a two-part window in the upper one. Inside are some 16th century paintings, a 13th century *Crucifix*, and a fine Byzantine-style *Virgin and Child*, also 13th century, in the chapter house.

The church of San Frediano.

Palazzo dell'Orologio.

PIAZZA DEI CAVALIERI

 The site of the forum in Roman Pisa, in medieval Pisa the square came to be known as Piazza delle Sette Vie (Square of the Seven Roads) because it stood at the crossroad of seven major arteries. During the Middle Ages, it was surrounded by Gothic buildings one of which, the *Gualandi Tower*, is now incorporated into the 17th century **Palazzo dell'Orologio**.

In 1561 Grand Duke Cosimo I dei Medici had the square altered to make room for several buildings he was having built for the Order of the Knights of Santo Stefano which he himself had recently founded. A 16th century *statue of Grand Duke Cosimo* stands by the fountain in front of Palazzo Cavalieri.

THE CHURCH OF SANTO STEFANO DEI CAVALIERI

 This imposing building was erected in 1569 by Giorgio Vasari over a pre-existing church. Actually, the façade was put up a

The church of Santo Stefano dei Cavalieri.

few years before Vasari's project got underway. On either side are low structures, once used by the members of the order as dressing rooms, which, in the 17th century, were transformed into the church aisles.

THE INTERIOR

The great nave is reached by way of four doors leading from the aisles.

The pair of fine holy *water basins* were designed by Vasari and executed by Chiarissimo Fancelli. The walls are hung with war trophies, including some fascinating *Turkish flags*.

The six paintings illustrating episodes from the *history of the Knights of Santo Stefano* on the impressive gilded wooden ceiling are by 16th century Tuscan painters of the Mannerist School.

Palazzo dei Cavalieri.

The grisaille scenes from the *life of St. Stephen* painted in tempera on the walls and attributed to Vasari, are of particular interest.

The main altar is an elaborate late 17th Baroque work by Francesco Silvani and Gian Battista Foggini.

THE PALAZZO DEI CAVALIERI

 This building was once known as Palazzo della Carovana (Palace of the Carovan), since here would-be knights of Santo Stefano attended a special initiation course called "caravan" (from the Persian word for voyage or company). During the Middle Ages, it served as the Palazzo degli Anziani del Popolo (a government building) and, like the church, was remodelled by Vasari in 1562. The lovely relief decoration of the facade, restored in the early 1900s, is original. In the niches between the third and fourth stories are *busts of the Medici grand dukes*. The building is presently the prestigious Scuola Normale Superior, a highly selective university, whose graduates, such as the physicist Enrico Fermi, not unrarely reach positions of great prominence.

Opposite are two 17th century buildings, **Palazzo del Collegio Puteano**, which incorporates the tiny **church of San Rocco** and the **Palazzo del Consiglio dell'Ordine**. The street off the southwest corner of the square facing Palazzo Cavalieri leads to the 11th century **church of San Sisto**.

The statue of Cosimo I de'Medici by Pietro Francavilla.

Back on Piazza dei Cavalieri, we walk past the façade of the church and take Via Dini on the right. We continue the whole length of Via Dini until reaching **Borgo Stretto**, one of the oldest and most picturesque streets in the city, lined with shops, arcades, and the palaces of Pisa's old noble families. Almost at the end is the **church of San Michele in Borgo**, dating from the 10th century. The façade marks the change from Pisan Romanesque to Gothic which took place at the beginning of the 14th century. Inside are traces of the frescoes which once covered all of the wall space and a fine 14th century Pisan *Crucifix*.

Borgo Stretto leads us back to Piazza Garibaldi. Here we turn left

The façade of the Palazzo dei Cavalieri.

into Lungarno Mediceo and continue down to the next square, Piazza Cairoli, where we make another left into Via Cavour. At the very beginning (right side) is the 11th century **church of San Pierino**, or **San Pietro in Vinculis** (St. Peter in Chains) which has a simple façade characterized by three-part windows surmounting unadorn portals. Inside there are some fine sculpted capitals, fragments of

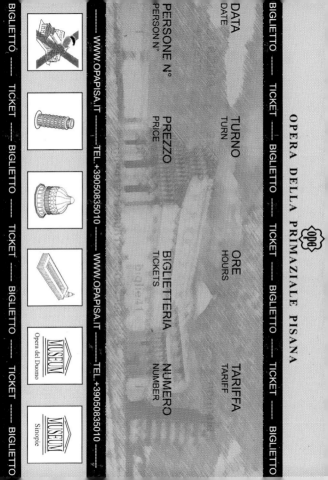

OPERA DELLA PRIMAZIALE PISANA

OPAP

BIGLIETTO —— TICKET —— BIGLIETTO —— TICKET —— BIGLIETTO —— TICKET —— BIGLIETTO

DATA
DATE

PERSONE N°
PERSON N°

TURNO
TURN

ORE
HOURS

PREZZO
PRICE

TARIFFA
TARIFF

BIGLIETTERIA
TICKETS

NUMERO
NUMBER

WWW.OPAPISA.IT —— TEL.+390508350 10

WWW.OPAPISA.IT —— TEL.+390508350 10

Opera del Duomo
MUSEUM

MUSEUM
Sinopie

BIGLIETTO —— TICKET —— BIGLIETTO —— TICKET —— BIGLIETTO —— TICKET —— BIGLIETTO

mosaic flooring, remains of 13th century frescoes, and an interesting, extremely old, crypt.

Continuing down Via Cavour, after a few blocks, we come to the **church of San Paolo all'Orto** on the square of the same name.

Although this 12th century church was greatly altered in the 1500s, its original capitals have survived intact. Making a right after leaving San Paolo immediately brings us to **Via San Francesco**. Here we turn left and continue to the square and church of the same name.

THE CHURCH OF SAN FRANCESCO

Work on the church got underway in the 13th century Giovanni Di Simone, the architect of the Camposanto building, is also responsible for the daring design of the bell-tower, two sides of which rest on huge blocks. The simple façade was erected in the 16th century.

THE INTERIOR

The aisleless nave is covered by a beamed ceiling. On the fourth altar on the right side is a 16th century painting of *St. Francis* by Santi di Tito. The frescoes of *saints* in the sacristy were painted in the late 15th century by Taddeo di Bartolo. In the **Chapter Room**, reached by crossing the cioister, are frescoes of the *Passion* by Pietro Gerini, dated 1392, which clearly reveal the influence of the Sienese School and the Florentine painter, Orcagna.

Turning right into Via Berlinghieri after leaving San Francesco, we make a left into Via San Lorenzo and go straight until reaching a huge tree-shaded square, **Piazza Martiri della Libertà**

The interior of the church of San Francesco.

The church of Santa Caterina.

On the northwest side is the church of Santa Caterina.

two rows of Gothic loggias. *Busts of saints* (1320) adorn a rose-window completed in the modern era.

THE CHURCH OF SANTA CATERINA

The façade is a typical example of 13th century Pisan architecture. The lower level has three arches with a portal beneath the central one, above which are

THE INTERIOR

Inside this aisleless church covered by a beamed ceiling are a number of art treasures. On the left side is a painting of the *Triumph of St. Thomas* attributed to Francesco Traini or Lippo Memmi (1363) and the *tomb of Archbishop Saltarelli* by Nino Pisano (1342). The *Angel*

81

Gabriel and *Virgin Annunciate* on either side of the altar are also by Nino.

To the north of the church lies the area that was once Roman Pisa, but unfortunately few vestiges of it are extant today. Taking Via San Zeno to the right of Santa Caterina brings us to the 11th century **church of San Zeno**. Built over the ruins of a Roman temple, but recently restored, San Zeno now sports its original tufa façade adorned with two-part windows and a porch.

Retracing our steps in to direction of Santa Caterina, we turn into Via Santa Caterina opposite the church, and continue right along Via Carducci until we come to the ruins of the **Roman Baths**. Erroneously called "Nero's Baths," they were actually built under the reign of Trajan.

Retracing our steps back to Piazza San Francesco, we make a right into Via Sighieri and then a left into Via del Giardino which leads into Piazza delle Gondole. Here we turn right into Via Santa Marta and continue down it to the Museo di San Matteo.

The church of San Zeno.

The cloister of Museo di S. Matteo.

THE MUSEO NAZIONALE DI S. MATTEO

The museum occupies thirty-eight rooms, formerly belonging to an old Benedictine monastery, restored and remodelled in 1949. The collection was started in the 18th century by Mons. Zucchetti and left to the Cathedral Board of Directors in 1796. Over the years, works from suppressed monasteries and convents and numerous private bequests con-

Crucifix by Giunta Pisano.
Opposite page: ***Crucifix*** by Berlinghieri.

tributed to the collection's growth.
Today, the visitor can arrive at a
good understanding of how art
developed in Pisa by carefully following it in chronological order.

CRUCIFIX BY GIUNTA PISANO

Giunta Pisano was born near
Pisa at the beginning of the 13th
century and was active between

1229 and 1254. Only a tiny number of Giunta Pisano'works exist in the world. This particular painting in the Pisa National Museum (which incidentally is one of the few signed) is a splendid expression, or interpretation if you will, of profound dramatic tension It characterizes Pisano as one of the greatest of the Romanesque painters, and the most masterly interpreter of Christ the Man, the man who suffers with the greatest humility and realism (*Christus Patiens*).

CRUCIFIX BY BERLINGHIERI

Berlinghiero Berlinghieri, the master painter from Lucca, may be considered the ideal interpreter of the *Christus Triumphans*. A 13th century artist, he looked back to the highly spiritual tradition of Byzantine art with its mysticism and stern asceticism. The work on display in the National Museum, conveys a strong feeling of purification and spirituality.

THE MADONNA DEL LATTE

In the "Madonna del Latte" Nino Pisano was dominated by a feeling for the delicacy of form and by his basically Gothic nature. This means: curving position of the Virgin, dynamism of form, and a hint of a smile on the Virgin's face. In effect, Nino was influenced more by Giovanni Pisano than by his own father Andrea. The "Madonna del Latte," Nino's masterpiece, was executed during the first half of the 14th century.for the Church of Santa Maria della Spina. Its refined elegance is typical of the balanced moderation of the Tuscan, and in particular, Pisan sculptural styles. The serene and almost cheerful expression on the Virgin's face and the highly spiritual feeling are revealed through a balance of lines repeated almost infinitely in the extremely sensitive work of Nino Pisano, Pisa's most delicate and human artist.

ST. PAUL

The real name of Masaccio, the young painter who worked in Pisa in 1426, was Tommaso di Messer Guidi. The altarpiece which he painted for the Church of the Carmine in Pisa was dismembered and ended up in five different museums: the National Gallery of London, the Lanckoronsky Collection in Vienna, the Friedrich Museum in Berlin, the National Museum of Naples, and the National Museum of Pisa. The St. Paul which remained in Pisa is possibly the most expressive figure in the whole work. Masaccio's fertile, tempestuous artistic talent reached its fulfilment in this balanced yet forceful figure. Unfortunately, the painter's development goes no further than 1428 when he died at the age of 27.

Masaccio boldly shook off the shackles of the decadent Gothic style, imposing his art with all the ardor of the new artistic wave of which he was the leader. In fact he is considered the greatest artist in the post-Gothic pre-Renaissance transition period. While it would be hard to pick out artists who specifically influenced him, we may mention the Florentine architect Filippo Brunelleschi whose a way of using perspective reappears in several painters' works. The St. Paul in the National Museum through his powerful, monumental appearance, expresses an inner charge of deep humanity which transcends the typical symbolism and idealization of the late Gothic style. The figure of St. Paul thus becomes an early representative of the realistic approach, almost revolutionary in the way Masaccio treats his subject as a man of the people and, as such, authentic and real, St. Paul in Masaccio's eyes is, in the first place a man of his times and secondly a glorious saint It is by being faithful to his own times that man can reveal the importance of his earthly journey in the reality of a dawning new age.

The Madonna del Latte by Nino Pisano.

St. Paul by Masaccio.

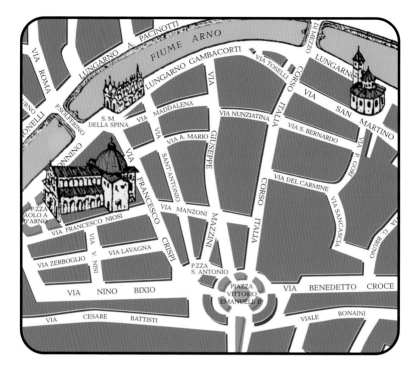

 Ponte di Mezzo

 Church of
Santa Maria
della Spina

 Palazzo
Gambacorti

Domus
Galilaeana

 Logge di Banchi

 Arsenal

 Church of
Santo Sepolcro

 Church of
San Paolo a
Ripa d'Arno

Crossing the Ponte di Mezzo to the left bank, we find ourselves in Piazza XX Settembre. The square contains two monuments, Palazzo Gambacorti, whose façade faces the Arno, and the Logge di Banchi.

crenellation, but it was torn down when Pisa came under Florentine rule. Remains of Roman columns are visible in the inner courtyard of the palace. Palazzo Gambacorti now serves as the Pisa City Hall.

THE PALAZZO GAMBACORTI

This grandiose, yet elegant, mansion was built for a Pisan nobleman, Pietro Gambacorti, between 1370 and 1380. Originally the building was topped by Ghibelline

THE LOGGE DI BANCHI

The Logge di Banchi was commissioned by Grand duke Ferdinando I dei Medici in the early 1600s. It was built by Cosimo Pugliani, although the design is

The church of Santo Sepolcro.

The interior of the church of Santo Sepolcro.

Buontalenti's, as a wool and silk market.

Taking Lungarno Galilei from Piazza XX Settembre, after a few blocks, we come to a little square with the church of Santo Sepolcro on the east side.

of the Baptistry, to build Santo Sepolcro around the middle of the 12th century. The octagonal building has the appearance of a solid construction, with a plain façade broken up only by undivided windows and three portals. A pyramidal cusp surmounts the whole.

THE CHURCH OF SANTO SEPOLCRO

The Templar Knights commissioned Diotisalvi, the architect

THE INTERIOR

The eight pillars which create an ambulatory around the apse support the dome resting upon elegant pointed arches. The central plan is like that of the Templars' churches in the Holy Land. Beneath the altar is the *tomb of Maria Mancini Colonna*, the favorite mistress of Louis XIV, the French Sun King, and niece of Cardinal Mazzarino, who died in Pisa in 1715.

Leaving the church we head in the direction away from the river towards Via San Martino. Taking Via San Martino on the left, we proceed until reaching the square and church of the same name.

THE CHURCH OF SAN MARTINO

The building dates from 1332, but was much altered in the 17th century. The lower part of the façade, with the typical Pisan arcading and three portals, is original.

La facciata della chiesa di Santa Maria della Spina.

THE INTERIOR

The entrance wall of the aisle-less interior is covered with 14th century frescoes by Giovanni di Nicola recounting the *childhood of Christ*. Above the door leading to the Cappella del Sacramento is a relief of *St. Martin and the Beggar*, sculpted by Andrea da Pontedera. Inside the chapel are frescoes by Antonio Veneziano. On the left is a 13th century *Crucifix* and a *Virgin and Child* sculpted by Andrea Guardi (late 15th century).

THE CHURCH OF SANTA MARIA DELLA SPINA

This tiny building, erected in 1323, is a jewel of Pisan Gothic architecture. Its name derives from a reliquary containing a thorn (spina), supposedly from Christ's Crown of Thorns, once preserved inside. The building originally stood on the river bank but, constantly threatened by floods and

The contours of the church of Santa Maria della Spina seen from the Lungarno.

The interior of Santa Maria della Spina.
Opposite page: **Portrait of Galilco Galilci** by Sustermans.

humidity, it was dismantled and set up on a safer spot at street level.

The exterior of the marble-faced church is elaborately decorated, especially the side facing the Arno. The 13 tabernacles on the upper section of the building contain statues of *Christ* and the *12 Apostles*, attributed to followers of Giovanni Pisano. The whole building is crowned with intricately-carved spires, and pinnacles, as well as figures of *saints and angels*. The façade is adorned with two rose-windows and three cusps. In the tabernacle in the middle are sculptures of the *Virgin and Child* and two *angels* by Giovanni di Balduccio. The altar inside the building has sculptures by Tommaso Pisano.

Past the church of Santa Maria della Spina, we come to the Ponte Solferino which we cross, immediately making a right into Lungarno Pacinotti. At Via San Nicola we make a left, go under an arch, and come out in Via Santa Maria, an

elegant thoroughfare where many of the university buildings are located. Immediately on our right we note the **church of San Nicola**. Little has been retained, however, of its original 12th century appearance. Despite its slight tilt, the belltower, an eightsided structure on a cyclindrical base, is quite lovely. Inside the church are a wooden

Crucifix, attributed to Giovanni Pisano, and a *Virgin and Child*, also wood, by Nino Pisano.

We continue down Via Santa Maria until reaching the **Domus Galilaeana** on the righthand side. A center for studies on Galileo and a museum of mementos of the great scientist, it was founded in 1941. Opposite is the **Museum of**

Natural History, whose zoological and paleontological collections are especially outstanding.

Retracing our steps back towards the river, we continue along it on the right until reaching the **Arsenale delle Galee** (Galley Shipyard) which was commissioned in the 16th century by the Knights of Santo Stefano. A bit farther down is the **Citadel**, a 15th century fortress built by Florentines for the defense of the precious shipyards.

Crossing back to the left bank by way of the Ponte della Cittadella,

we turn left and, passing the **Porta a Mare**, a city gate, we soon come to Piazza San Paolo a Ripa d'Arno and the church of the same name.

THE CHURCH OF SAN PAOLO A RIPA D'ARNO

This superb example of Pisan Romanesque architecture was actually founded in the 9th century. Over the centuries it has

The Citadel dominated by the thirteenth century Guelf Tower.

been remodelled several times (The most recent restoration dates from 1943). Its typically Pisan façade, with a lower section of arcading topped by three tows of loggias, is faced in striped marble.

THE INTERIOR

The church's single aisles are set off from the nave by granite columns with splendid capitals. Above the choir is a huge dome On the right is the *tomb of Burgundio*, made out of a Roman sarcophagus. In the left aisle is a painting of the *Virgin and Child with saints*, dated 1397, by Turino Vanni.

Behind the church, in the middle of the lawn, is the tiny **Chapel of St. Agatha**, built in the 12th cen-

The church of San Paolo a Ripa d'Arno.

The octagonally shaped Chapel of St. Agatha.

tury and attributed to Diotisalvi. The sole decorative motifs on the plain octagonal brick building are the three-part windows on four sides and the corbel table running around the giant cusp.

ENVIRONS OF PISA

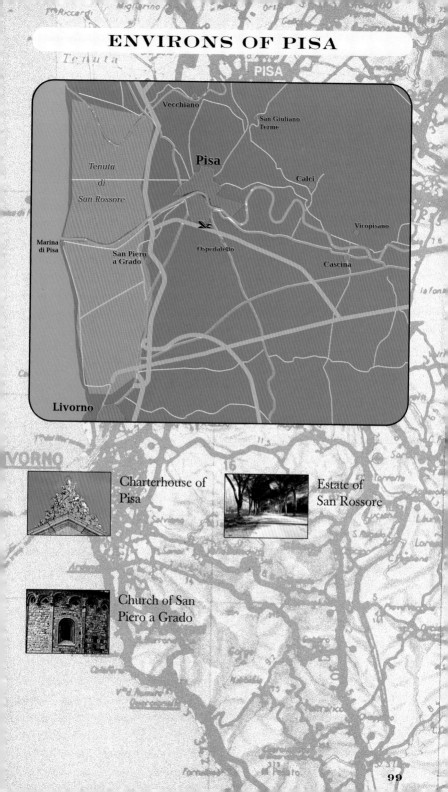

Charterhouse of Pisa

Estate of San Rossore

Church of San Piero a Grado

CHARTERHOUSE OF PISA

Less than 9 miles from Pisa, in a little town named Calci, is the Charterhouse of Pisa, which ranks as the second largest in Italy after that of Pavia. Its setting is breathtaking. Although founded in 1336, its present appearance dates from the late 18th century when it was remodelled by Nicola Stassi.

The complex includes the monks'cells, a *church*, and several cloisters, among them the magnificent **Chiostro Grande**. The church was originally built in the last quarter of the 14th century, but considerably altered in the 17th century. It is aisleless and divided into two sections by a colored marble rood-screen. The 17th century frescoes depict *scenes from the Old Testament*. Of note are the 15th century choir stalls and a 17th century *angel*, by followers of Bernini.

The church façade of the Charterhouse of Pisa.

THE CHURCH OF SAN PIERO A GRADO

Located about 3 miles from Pisa, the basilica is well worth a visit. The sight of this masterpiece of Pisan Romanesque rising majestic and solemn in the open countryside is well worth the trip. The church is characterized by the linearity of its design and simplicity of its forms, not to mention its utter lack of a façade. In fact, it has three apses on the east side and one on the west the entrance being a doorway cut into the north side. It was built around the middle of the 11th century over a pre-existing 6th century basilica.

Throughout the Middle Ages, San Piero was a very popular place of worship, since St. Peter supposedly stopped off here on his way from Antioch to Rome in 44 A.D.

THE INTERIOR

The spacious and lovely interior has single aisles delineated by a double row of columns with Roman capitals. The decoration is sober and reduced to the bare minimum: the round arches have red and white stripes and the walls of the nave are frescoed with scenes of the *life of St. Peter* between a row of *portraits of popes* and the *Walls of the Heavenly City*. The frescoes were painted in the early 1300s by Deodato Orlandi.

The basilica of San Piero a Grado.

A view of the lush vegetation in the San Rossore forest.

THE ESTATE OF SAN ROSSORE

This huge estate is mostly woodland covered with Mediterranean pine trees, oaks, and other typical flora of the Mediterranean region. The animals which roam it - deer, wild boar, rare species of birds, and even dromedaries - are descendants of the first specimans brought to San Rossore by Grand Duke Ferdinand II in the 17th century.

In the 16th century the estate was ceded to Alessandro dei Medici by the deacons of the Cathedral of Pisa. Successively, it was passed on to the Lorraine grand dukes and then to the Savoys, the Italian royal family. Now the estate, property of the President of Italy, is currently being turned into a National Park.

USEFUL INFORMATION

DISTANCES (KM) FROM THE MAIN ITALIAN CITIES

	Bari	Bologna	Florence	Genoa	Milan	Naples	Rome	Turin	Venice
Pisa	810	180	95	155	275	580	325	325	330

dialing code for Pisa: 050

TOURIST INFORMATION BUREAUS

- via Benedetto Croce 26 ☎ 40096/40202 **Fax** 40903
- piazza del Duomo ☎ 560464
- piazza della Stazione ☎ 42291
- Aeroporto G. Galilei ☎ 500707

TRAINS:
Stazione Pisa Centrale
☎ 1478-88088

PLANES:
Aeroporto G. Galilei
☎ 3061700

TAXIS:
Radio Taxi	☎ 541600
Piazza Stazione	☎ 41252
Piazza Duomo	☎ 561878
Aeroporto	☎ 28542
Piazza Garibaldi	☎ 580000

CAR HIRE:
ACI-Liberty rent
Aeroporto G. Galilei
☎ (050)48088/49500

Autonoleggio Toscano
via Bonaini 125 ☎ 46127

Avis
Aeroporto G. Galilei ☎ 42028

Budget Italy by Car
Aeroporto G. Galilei ☎ 45490

Eurodollar
Aeroporto G. Galilei
☎ 46209/48138

Europcar
Aeroporto G. Galilei ☎ 42028

Hertz
Aeroporto G. Galilei
☎ 43220/49187

Maggiore
Aeroporto G. Galilei ☎ 42574

Pa. Car Service
Aeroporto G. Galilei ☎ 46318

Pittore
Aeroporto G. Galilei ☎ 49259

Program
Aeroporto G. Galilei ☎ 500296

EMERGENCY PHONE NUMBERS

☎

Police Emergency............113
Police (Headquarters):
via Lalli................................**583511**
Municipal Police:
via del Moro...........**50144/502626**
Carabinieri:
Emergency.............................**112**
Carabinieri (Headquarters):
via G. da Pisa, 1.................**541900**
Emergency Road Service ACI
(Automobile Club)................**116**
Ambulance.............................**118**
First Aid...........................**554433**
Hospitals:
-Santa Chiara
via Roma, 67......................**592111**
-Cisanello
via Paradisa,2.....................**592111**
-Calambrone
viale del Tirreno, 64..........**592111**
City of Pisa:
Piazza XX Settembre..........**910111**
City hall.............................**910111**

Baptistry, piazza del Duomo
☎ 560547/561820
hours, winter: 9.00 a.m.- sunset
hours, summer: 8.00 a.m.- 7.40 p.m.
closed on 1/1, 25/12

Camposanto Vecchio, piazza del
Duomo ☎ 560547/561820
hours, winter: 9.00 a.m.- sunset
hours, summer: 8.00 a.m.- 7.40 p.m.
closed on 1/1, 25/12

Cattedrale, piazza del Duomo
☎ 560547/561820
hours, winter: 7.45 a.m.-1.00 p.m.
and 3.00 p.m.- sunset
April-October: 10.00 a.m.-7.40
p.m. (weekdays)
1.00 p.m.-7.40 p.m. (holidays)

**Fortezza Nuova and
Giardino Rosselmini-Scotto,**
l.no Fibonacci ☎ 23044
Jan., Nov., Dec.: 8.00 a.m.-5.00 p.m.
Feb., March: 8.00 a.m.-5.30 p.m
Oct., April: 8.00 a.m.-7.00 p.m
May, Sept.: 8.00 a.m.-8.00 p.m
June, July, Aug.: 8.00 a.m.-8.30 p.m
closed 1/1, Easter, 1/5, 25/12

Museo dell'Opera del Duomo,
piazza Arcivescovado, 8
☎ 560547/561820
hours, winter: 9.00 a.m.- sunset
hours, summer: 8.00 a.m.- 7.40 p.m.
closed on 1/1, 25/12

Museo delle Sinopie, piazza del
Duomo ☎ 560547/561820
hours, winter: 9.00 a.m.- sunset
hours, summer: 8.00 a.m.- 7.40 p.m.
closed on 1/1, 25/12

**Museo Nazionale di Palazzo
Reale,** lung.no Pacinotti, 46
☎ 926539
hours, weekdays: 9.00 a.m.-2.00 p.m.

Museo Nazionale di San Matteo,
lung.no Mediceo ☎ 541865
hours, weekdays: 9.00 a.m.-7.00p.m.
hours, holidays: 9.00 a.m.-1.00p.m.
closed Mondays, 1/1, 1/5, 15/8, 25/12

Botanical Gardens
via L. Ghini, 5
☎ 560045/561795
hours: Monday-Friday 8.00 a.m.-
1.00/2.00 p.m.-5.30 p.m.
Saturdays 8.00 a.m.-1.00 p.m.
closed Sundays and holidays

**Parco Naturale di Migliarino-
San Rossore-Massaciuccoli
and Tenuta di San Rossore,**
Ente Parco Regionale, via Aurelia
Nord, 4 ☎ 525211

****

D'Azeglio
piazza V. Emanuele II, 18b — **Fax.** 28017 ☎ 500310
Grand Hotel Duomo
via S. Maria, 94 — **Fax.** 560418 ☎ 561894
Jolly Hotel Cavalieri
piazza della Stazione, 2 — **Fax.** 502242 ☎ 43290

***

Ariston
via Cardinale Maffi, 42 — **Fax.** 561891 ☎ 561834
Capitol
via E. Fermi, 13 — **Fax.** 27168 ☎ 49597
Europa Park Hotel
via Andrea Pisano, 23 — **Fax.** 554930 ☎ 500732
Francesco
via S. Maria, 139 — **Fax.** 556145 ☎ 554109
La Pace
viale A. Gramsci, Gall. B — **Fax.** 502266 ☎ 48863
Minerva
piazza Toniolo, 20 — **Fax.** 501559 ☎ 501081
Roma
via Bonanno Pisano, 111 — **Fax.** 550164 ☎ 554488
Royal Victoria
lungarno Pacinotti, 12 — **Fax.** 940180 ☎ 940111
Terminus e Plaza
via Colombo, 45 — **Fax.** 500303 ☎ 500303
Touring
via Puccini, 24 — **Fax.** 502148 ☎ 46374
Verdi
piazza della Repubblica, 5 — **Fax.** 598947 ☎ 598947
Villa Kinzica
piazza Arcivescovado, 2 — **Fax.** 551204 ☎ 560419

**

Amalfitana
via Roma, 44 — **Fax.** 25218 ☎ 29000
Bologna
via Mazzini, 57 — **Fax.** 43070 ☎ 502120
Cecile
via Roma, 54 — **Fax.** 29515 ☎ 29328

HOTELS

Di Stefano
via S. Apollonia, 35   **Fax.** 556038   ☎ 553559

La Torre
via C. Battisti, 17   **Fax.** 589066   ☎ 25220

Milano
via Mascagni, 14   **Fax.** 44237   ☎ 23162

Moderno
via Corridoni, 103   **Fax.** 49208   ☎ 25021

Pisa
via Manzoni, 22   ☎ 44551

Roseto
via Mascagni, 24   **Fax.** 42596   ☎ 42596

Villa Primavera
via Bonanno Pisano, 43   **Fax.** 27020   ☎ 23537

*

Clio
via S. Lorenzino, 3   ☎ 28446

Galileo
via S. Maria, 12   **Fax.** 40621   ☎ 40621

Giardino
piazza Manin, 1   ☎ 562101

Gronchi
piazza Arcivescovado, 1   ☎ 561823

Helvetia
via G. Boschi, 31   ☎ 553084

Rinascente
via del Castelletto, 28   ☎ 580460

Serena
via Cavalca, 45   **Fax.** 580809   ☎ 580809

RESIDENCES

Isola Verde
via Bargagna, 44   **Fax.** 584628   ☎ 575711

CAMPINGS

Torre Pendente
viale delle Cascine, 86   **Fax.** 561734   ☎ 561704

77, via S. Lorenzo, 69 ☎ 540160
Al Banco della Berlina, piazza dei Facchini, 13 ☎ 28461
Alla Giornata, via S. Bibbiana, 11 ☎ 542504
Alle Bandierine, via Mercanti, 4 ☎ 500000
Antista, piazza Guerrazzi, 4 ☎ 540160
Antonietta, via S. Maria, 179 ☎ 561810
Asmara, via C. Cammeo, 27 ☎ 552711
Azzurra, via M. Nelli, 10 ☎ 562083
Beny, piazza Chiara Gambacorti, 22 ☎ 25067
Bruno, via Luigi Bianchi, 12 ☎ 560818
Buffet Stazione, piazza Stazione, 12 ☎ 46319
Capriccio Pub, via Matteucci, 50 ☎ 542089
Cassio, piazza Cavallotti, 14 ☎ 553469
Cagliostro, via del Castelletto, 12 ☎ 598555
Centrale, piazza Vittorio Emanuele, 22 ☎ 20457
Charleston, via C. Colombo, 67 ☎ 501039
Charlie, via Bonanno, 53/a ☎ 43403
China Town (chinese), via C. Matilde, 6/8 ☎ 563378
Cirano, via Roma, 52 ☎ 48513
Ciucci, via S. Maria, 163 ☎ 561976
Cucciolo, via S. Bernardo ☎ 29435
Da Matteo, via l'Arancio, 46 ☎ 41057
Da Poldino, via delle Cascine Vecchie, 13 ☎ 531763
Dab, via S. Bernardo, 20 (closed on Wednesdays) ☎ 500872
David, via Mercanti, 25 ☎ 542592
Del Borgo, via Case Dipinte, 2 ☎ 542622
Di là d'Arno, lung.no Gambacorti, 10 ☎ 49250
Duomo, via Roma, 70 ☎ 562352
Duomo (hotel), via S. Maria, 94 ☎ 561894
Emilio, via C. Cammeo, 44 ☎ 562096
Francesco, via CS. Maria, 129 ☎ 555453
Giardino, piazza Manin, 1 ☎ 562101
Gino, piazza Vittorio Emanuele, 19 ☎ 23437
Il Bistrot, lung.no Medìceo, 66 ☎ 542430
Il Boccone, via Roma, 42 ☎ 27275
Il Borghetto, via del Borghetto, 5 ☎ 574734
Il Braciere, via XXIV Maggio, 94 ☎ 564028
Il Cacciatore, via del Carmine, 34 ☎ 42338
Il Campano, via Cavalca, 44 ☎ 580585
Il Canguro, via S. Maria, 151 ☎ 561942

RESTAURANTS

Il Cavaliere (hotel), p.za della Stazione, 2 ☎ 43290
Il Cavallino, via S. Lorenzo, 66 ☎ 555366
Il Coccio, via S. Maria, 105 ☎ 562727
Il Fagiolo, via S. Lorenzo, 43 ☎ 27336
Il Mago di Oz, via del Borghetto, 40 ☎ 576390
Il Montino, vicolo del Monte, 1 ☎ 598695
Il Nodo Piano, via S. Paolo, 62/64 ☎ 49871
Il Nuraghe, via Mazzini, 58 ☎ 44368
Il Paiolo, via Curtatone e Montanara, 9 ☎ 42528
Il Podere, via Arelia Sud, 12 ☎ 960127
Il Pomo d'Oro, via La Nunziatina, 13 ☎ 500015
Il Ristoro della Faggiola, via della Faggiola, 1 ☎ 552725
Il Rompicapo, via B. Croce, 59 ☎ 48238
Il Turista, p.za dell'Arcivescovado, 17 ☎ 560932
Il Vecchio Dado, lung.no Pacinotti, 21 ☎ 580900
Il Viale, viale Bonaini, 78 ☎ 26016
Ivano-Crazy House, via del Brennero, 34 ☎ 564700
Kostas (Greek), via del Borghetto, 39 ☎ 571467
L'Europeo, via S. Maria, 177 ☎ 560531
L'Osteria di Marvin, via L. Bianchi, 33/37 ☎ 564938
La Buca, via Queirolo, 25 ☎ 24130
La Buca, via Galli Tassi, 6/b ☎ 560660
La Cereria, via Pietro Gori, 33 ☎ 20336
La Draga, p.za Don Minzoni, 5 ☎ 24620
La Grotta, via S. Francesco, 103 ☎ 578105
La Leccornia, p.za C. Gambacorti, 41 ☎ 26086
La Luna Rossa, via C.Cattaneo, 125 ☎ 41015
La Mescita, via Cavalca, 2 ☎ 598667
La Muraglia (chinese), via Toselli, 1 ☎ 27372
La Pergoletta, via delle Belle Torri ☎ 542458
La Piedigrotta, p.za Garibaldi, 6 ☎ 542253
La Sapienza, via San Frediano, 21 ☎ 20503
La Scaletta, via Pietrasantina, 107 ☎ 562269
La Spigolatrice, via Cagliari, 25 ☎ 563151
La Stanzina, via Cavalca, 30 ☎ 570200
La Tana, via San Frediano, 6 ☎ 580540
La Vecchia Pisa, via S. Maria, 111 ☎ 501592
Le Giare, via Vecchia Tramvia, 10 ☎ 983329
Manredo, via C. Cammeo, 43 ☎ 562315
Maria, via Fiorentina, 461 ☎ 980135

RESTAURANTS

Marino, via Bonaini, 119 ☎ 42157
Mediceo, lung.no Mediceo, 53 ☎ 541080
Michele, viale Bonaini, 98/100 ☎ 24128
Moisé, via Bonaini, 121 ☎ 29528
Nuovo Olimpionico, via Pietrasantina, 16 ☎ 562341
Okay, via Carducci, 53 ☎ 553061
Oriente (chinese), via C. Cammeo, 66 ☎ 554814
Osteria dei Cavalieri, via San Frediano, 16 ☎ 580858
Osteria Porton Rosso, vicolo Porton Rosso ☎ 580566
Pechino (chinese), via A. Pisano, 122 ☎ 532427
Piccolo Mondo, via C. Colombo, 63 ☎ 27129
Pick a Flower, via Serafini, 14 ☎ 42561
Pub 2A, via Garibaldi, 89 ☎ 573160
Punto e Basta, via Lucchese, 33/b ☎ 562730
Renzo, via Garibaldi, 214 ☎ 570077
Rino, via Aurelia Nord, 36 ☎ 532572
Ristoro dei Vecchi Macelli, via Volturno, 49 ☎ 20424
S. Francisco, vicolo del Tinti, 26 ☎ 580240
Salza, Borgo Stretto, 44 ☎ 580144
Santa Maria, via S. Maria 114/116 ☎ 561881
Schiaccianoci, via Vespucci, 104/a ☎ 21024
Turiddo, p.za S. Frediano, 12 ☎ 580600
Ungherese, via Lucchese, 5 ☎ 564579
Vecchio Teatro, via Collegio Ricci, 2 ☎ 20210

CINEMAS - THEATERS

Ariston, via Turati, 1
☎ 43407

Arno, via Conte Fazio
☎ 43289

Arsenale, via Scaramucci, 4
☎ 502640

Astra, corso Italia, 18
☎ 23075

Estivo Roma, via Piave, 47
☎ 552261

Lanteri, via S. M. Scalzi, 46
☎ 577100

Mignon, lung.no Pacinotti
☎ 580969

Teatro Nuovo, p.za Stazione, 1
☎ 41332

Teatro Odeon, p.za S.P. all'Orto, 18
☎ 540168

Teatro Verdi, via Palestro, 40
☎ 579560

CONTENTS